TANGIER
Travel Guide 2024

A Comprehensive Off the Beaten Path Guide to Culture, History, Hidden Gems and Top Attractions in Morocco's Underrated Paradise

Wendy T. Sierra

Copyright

All rights reserved. No part of this publication may be reproduced, distributed, or transmitted in any form or by any means, including photocopying, recording, or other electronic or mechanical methods, without the prior written permission of the owner.

©[2024][Wendy T. Sierra]

Table of Contents

Copyright	1
Table of Contents	2
Forward	3
Introduction	5
Planning Your Trip	11
Accommodation in Tangier	17
Must-See Attractions	23
Discovering Tangiers' Hidden Gems	29
Cultural Experiences	35
Day Trips & Excursions	41
Shopping in Tangiers	47
Culinary Delights of Tangier	54
Nightlife & Entertainment	62
Outdoor Activities & Adventures	68
Family-Friendly Activities	74
Wellness & Relaxation	81
Events & Festivals	88
Practical Information	95
Sample Itineraries	103
Conclusion	110

Forward

Embarking on a journey to Tangier is like stepping into a living storybook where the past and present merge seamlessly, creating a unique and vibrant atmosphere. As I write this foreword, I can't help but reminisce about my first encounter with this enchanting city. It was a balmy evening when I arrived in Tangier, the salty breeze from the Mediterranean brushing against my face. The city welcomed me with open arms, and from that moment, I knew I was in for an extraordinary adventure.

Tangier is a city of contrasts, where ancient Kasbahs sit alongside modern cafes, and bustling souks coexist with serene beaches. During my stay, I found myself constantly in awe of the city's dynamic energy. One of my most memorable experiences was wandering through the Medina's labyrinthine streets, where every corner seemed to whisper tales of the past. I stumbled upon a small spice shop, its shelves brimming with vibrant colors and intoxicating scents. The shopkeeper, an elderly man with a twinkle in his eye, shared stories of Tangier's history as we sipped on mint tea. It was in moments like these that I felt the soul of the city.

Tangier's cultural diversity is another aspect that captivated me. Sitting at a café in the Petit Socco, I observed locals and travelers alike, each adding their own flavor to the city's rich heritage. The call to prayer from nearby mosques mingled with the sounds of street musicians, creating a symphony that was both chaotic and beautiful. One evening, I attended a traditional Moroccan music performance, where the rhythms of the Gnawa musicians resonated deep within me, leaving an indelible mark on my spirit.

In this travel guide, I aim to share with you the magic of Tangier, from its must-see attractions to its hidden gems. Whether you're a history buff, a culture enthusiast, or simply looking for a place to unwind, Tangier has something to offer. My hope is that this guide will not only help you navigate the city but also inspire you to create your own unforgettable memories.

As you turn these pages, I invite you to immerse yourself in the essence of Tangier. May your journey be filled with discovery, adventure, and the same sense of wonder that I experienced. Welcome to Tangier – a city that promises to enchant and inspire.

Introduction

Tangier, Morocco's charming gateway to Africa, has captivated tourists, artists, and authors for ages. Tangier, located on the African continent's tip where the Mediterranean Sea meets the Atlantic Ocean, is a cultural melting pot, a historical city, and a site of spectacular beauty. Its intricate medina, lively souks, and gorgeous shoreline provide a sensory feast for all visitors. Tangier is a city that offers unique adventures at every turn, whether you're drawn to its historic history, dynamic present, or optimistic future.

Welcome to Tangier
When you arrive in Tangier by plane, boat, or rail, you are met by a city that feels both old and delightfully contemporary. Tangier's particular allure stems from its ability to perfectly merge the ancient with the contemporary. Ancient mosques and trendy cafés coexist, and traditional Moroccan handicraft is available alongside contemporary art galleries. This dynamic juxtaposition is what makes Tangier a must-see destination.

Tangier has always been a sanctuary for creatives, authors, and explorers. From Paul Bowles and the

Beat Generation to today's modern artists and musicians, Tangier has long served as a source of inspiration and innovation. It's a site where you may lose yourself in the medina's twisting lanes, experience the rich aromas of Moroccan food, and be immersed in the rhythms of native music and dancing.

Historical Overview

Tangier's history is as varied and extensive as the city itself. Its strategic location at the crossroads of Europe and Africa has made it a prized possession for several dynasties and civilizations. The Phoenicians built a trade post here in the 5th century BC, which is when the city was founded. Tangier's importance expanded during Roman administration, becoming a major hub of commerce and culture.

Tangier has been affected by a variety of civilizations throughout history, including Berbers, Carthaginians, Romans, Vandals, Byzantines, Arabs, Portuguese, Spanish, and French. Each of these civilizations has left an imprint on the city, adding to its distinct architectural and cultural fabric.

Tangier emerged as an international hub in the twentieth century, attracting a diverse population of expats, artists, and spies. The city's status as a free port, along with its image as a sanctuary for authors and bohemians, only contributed to its allure. Tangier's historical history is still preserved today through museums, monuments, and stories shared by its citizens.

Geographical Layout

Tangier's geographical arrangement is as interesting as its history. The city is situated on Morocco's northern coast, where the Mediterranean Sea meets the Atlantic Ocean. This strategic location provides breathtaking views of both bodies of water and the distant coast of Spain. The Strait of Gibraltar, one of the world's most important maritime crossings, is just to the north.

The city is constructed on a series of hills, which offer amazing panoramic views from various vantage points. The medina, or old city, is a tangle of small streets, busy marketplaces, and medieval structures. It is positioned on a hill overlooking the harbor and the sea, providing a gorgeous backdrop that has inspired innumerable painters and authors.

Beyond the medina, Tangier's modern metropolis sprawls with large boulevards, modern buildings, and beautiful gardens. The beachside promenade, known as the Corniche, is a popular destination for both locals and tourists, providing a lovely area to stroll and enjoy the sea air.

Climate and Ideal Time to Visit

Tangier's climate is one of its numerous draws, making it an excellent year-round resort. The city has a Mediterranean climate, which includes moderate, rainy winters and scorching, dry summers. However, its seaside position tempers the extremes, ensuring that even at the height of summer, temperatures remain comfortable.

Tangier is best visited in the **spring (March to May)** and **fall (September to November)**, when the weather is pleasant but not too hot and the city's gardens and parks are in blossom. During these seasons, you can experience the city's outdoor attractions and bustling street life without the hordes that arrive during the high summer months.

Tangier experiences warm winters, with daytime temperatures seldom dipping below 10°C (50°F). This makes it an ideal destination for anyone seeking to flee the severe winters of Europe and North America. Summer, while hotter, is still bearable due to the refreshing sea air.

Language & Culture

Tangier's cultural wealth is matched by its linguistic variety. Morocco's official language is Arabic, especially Moroccan Arabic (Darija). However, due to Tangier's historical ties and role as an international city, French and Spanish are also commonly spoken. English is becoming more widespread, notably in the tourist and hospitality industries.

The city's culture is a dynamic fusion of its many influences. Traditional Moroccan practices combine with European and African influences, resulting in a unique cultural mosaic. Tangier's music, art, and food embody this blend.

Music is an essential component of Tangier's cultural fabric. The city is well-known for its traditional Gnawa music, a spiritual and rhythmic form that originated in Sub-Saharan Africa. In addition to Gnawa, numerous events and venues in the city include Andalusian, Berber, and modern Moroccan music.

Tangier's food reflects its eclectic background, including tastes and ingredients from around the Mediterranean and beyond. Tangier offers a fantastic eating experience with fresh seafood, fragrant spices, and a diversity of influences. Make sure to taste local favorites including tagine, couscous, and pastilla.

In summary, Tangier is a city that captivates visitors with its history, geography, climate, language, and culture. Tangier, whether you're exploring its old alleyways, taking in the seaside vistas, or immersing yourself in its vivid customs, provides an incredible voyage into the heart of Morocco.

Planning Your Trip

Navigating the Gateway to Africa
Traveling to Tangier, Africa's captivating gateway, necessitates some preparation to ensure a pleasant and wonderful visit. This chapter provides complete advice on making your journey to Tangier as easy as possible. From selecting the best form of transportation to comprehending the local currency and safety precautions, we've got you covered. So, prepare to dig into the details of your vacation, allowing you to focus on enjoying every second of your stay in this wonderful city.

How to Get To Tangier
Getting to Tangier is an experience in and of itself, with a variety of travel options to suit all likes and budgets. **Tangier Ibn Battouta Airport (TNG)** is the key international gateway, with direct flights from major cities in Europe and the Middle East. Airlines including Royal Air Maroc, Ryanair, and Air Arabia run regular flights, making air travel a practical alternative.

For those who are already in Morocco or adjacent Spain, ferry services provide an intriguing option. Ferries from Tarifa, Algeciras, and Gibraltar in

Spain arrive in Tangier on a regular basis, transporting passengers directly to the city's Tangier Ville port. This gorgeous marine path is ideal for people who prefer a more relaxed pace.

Train aficionados will be glad to learn that Tangier is well connected to Morocco's enormous rail network. The high-speed Al Boraq train connects Tangier to important towns like Casablanca and Rabat, providing a comfortable and quick means of travel across the nation. Buses and private vehicle rentals are also available for individuals who prefer road travel, giving them flexibility and the opportunity to explore Morocco's countryside.

Visa and Travel Requirements

Before you pack your bags for Tangier, be sure you understand the visa and travel requirements. Citizens of several countries, including the United States, Canada, the European Union, and others, can enter Morocco without a visa for stays of up to 90 days. However, rules might change, so it's always a good idea to check with your local Moroccan consulate or embassy to see what the newest requirements are.

If you do require a visa, the process is rather simple. You must send an application form, a passport-sized picture, proof of lodging, and a return ticket. Processing timeframes might vary, so apply well ahead of your planned trip dates.

Additionally, be sure your passport is valid for at least six months after your intended departure date from Morocco. Travel insurance is also highly suggested since it may give peace of mind in the event of unforeseen incidents or crises.

Currency & Money Matters

Tangier's native currency is the Moroccan dirham (MAD). It is important to have some local money on hand upon arrival to cover urgent needs like transportation, gratuities, and minor purchases. ATMs are readily available in Tangier, and the majority accept foreign debit and credit cards, making it simple to withdraw cash as required.

Currency exchange services are also widely available, with locations at the airport, major hotels, and around the city. It is best to examine rates and fees before converting big quantities of money. Credit cards are generally accepted at hotels, restaurants, and larger stores, but it's always a good idea to bring extra cash for smaller places and markets.

Tipping is not required, although it is valued in Morocco. A 10-15% tip is usual at restaurants, and modest tips for hotel workers, guides, and taxi drivers are also appreciated.

Safety Tips for Travelers

Tangier is typically a safe location, but like with any city, it's best to take simple measures to guarantee a trouble-free trip. Petty theft, such as pickpocketing, can occur, particularly in congested locations like markets and tourist destinations. Keep your valuables safe, and be aware of your surroundings.

Dress modestly and respect local customs and traditions. This not only demonstrates cultural awareness, but it also allows you to blend in and avoid unwanted attention. Avoid wandering alone in new locations after dark, and instead choose trusted transit, such as official taxis or ridesharing services.

Scams targeting visitors are possible, so be aware of excessively pleasant persons who offer unwanted aid or services. It is usually a good idea to double-check information with your hotel or another reliable source.

To avoid gastrointestinal problems, make sure you get any essential immunizations before going and consume only bottled water. Pharmacies are well-stocked, however it is a good idea to bring any drugs you may require.

Useful Travel Apps & Resources

In today's digital age, using the correct travel applications may dramatically improve your Tangier experience. Here are some essential applications and tools for your trip:

- **Google Maps** is essential for navigating the city's meandering streets and locating sights, restaurants, and lodgings.
- **TripAdvisor** is a great place to find reviews and suggestions for Tangier hotels, restaurants, and attractions.
- **XE Currency** is useful for changing currencies and ensuring you obtain the best exchange rates.
- **Google Translate:** Although many individuals in Tangier know French, Spanish, or English, this program can assist overcome language barriers, particularly in Arabic.
- **Uber/Careem:** These ride-hailing applications are accessible in Tangier and

provide a simple and dependable method to move about the city.
- **HappyCow:** This app helps vegetarian and vegan visitors locate plant-based meal alternatives in Tangier.
- **Visit Morocco** is Morocco's official tourist app, which provides information on sights, events, and practical travel suggestions.

With these resources at your disposal, you'll be well-prepared to make the most of your trip to Tangier, guaranteeing a seamless and pleasurable tour from beginning to end.

In summary, organizing a trip to Tangier requires a combination of practical procedures and deliberate preparation. From choosing your means of transportation to knowing local traditions and currencies, every detail adds to a smooth and enjoyable travel experience. Armed with the necessary information and resources, you'll be able to confidently experience Tangier's enchantment and mystique.

Accommodation in Tangier

Finding Your Perfect Home Away from Home.
Tangier has a wide variety of lodgings to accommodate any traveler's needs and interests. Whether you want luxurious grandeur, quaint boutique hotels, or low-cost choices, this city offers it all. Tangier's hospitality industry offers everything from medieval riads to modern hotels and one-of-a-kind Airbnb apartments, ensuring that your stay is as memorable as the city itself. Let's look at the top locations to stay in this wonderful area.

Luxury Hotels

Tangier's luxury hotels are ideal for guests seeking elegance and world-class service. These places provide high-end amenities, breathtaking vistas, and great service to make your stay unforgettable.

Mandarin Oriental, Tangier: Located in the center of the city, this five-star hotel provides an oasis of peace with beautiful gardens, opulent rooms, and magnificent views of the Mediterranean Sea. The hotel's spa, exquisite dining options, and superb service create a sumptuous atmosphere.

La Maison Blanche: Located in the ancient Kasbah, this boutique hotel mixes traditional Moroccan architecture with modern luxury. Each room is distinctively furnished, combining elegance and comfort. The rooftop patio offers amazing views of both the city and the Strait of Gibraltar.

El Minzah Hotel: The El Minzah Hotel, a Tangier landmark with a rich history and timeless appeal. This five-star hotel, built in the 1930s, features magnificent rooms, a beautiful courtyard, and a well-known spa. Its central position gives it an excellent starting point for exploring the city.

Mid-Range Hotels

Travelers looking for comfort and convenience without breaking the budget can discover lots of great mid-range hotels in Tangier. These lodgings strike a decent compromise between quality and price, with comfortable rooms and a variety of services.

Hotel Rembrandt: This lovely hotel has comfortable rooms with contemporary conveniences, a refreshing pool, and is conveniently located between the beach and the medina. The hotel's restaurant delivers exquisite Moroccan and foreign food, making it an excellent choice for middle-class guests.

Dar Nour: Located in the Kasbah, Dar Nour is a beautifully renovated riad that combines traditional Moroccan decor with modern comfort. The rooftop patio offers breathtaking views of the city and sea, and the courteous staff promises a warm welcome.

Kenzi Solazur: This hotel overlooks Tangier Bay and has spacious accommodations, a wide outdoor pool, and a variety of eating options. Its great position between the beach and the city center makes it a good alternative for visitors who want to see Tangier's sights.

Budget-Friendly Options

Tangier also offers a selection of budget-friendly lodgings. These alternatives provide comfortable accommodations without sacrificing quality, enabling you to explore the city without straining your budget.

Hotel Mamora: Located in the center of the medina, Hotel Mamora provides clean and comfortable rooms at an affordable price. The hotel's balcony provides panoramic views of the city, and its central position allows you to explore Tangier's main attractions on foot.

The Medina Hostel is ideal for backpackers and lone travelers, offering dormitory-style and private rooms at reasonable rates. The social rooms allow you to meet other tourists, and the staff may organize trips and activities.

Hotel Continental: A historic hotel with affordable rates, Hotel Continental provides modest yet comfortable rooms with breathtaking views of the bay. Its central position near the medina and ferry port makes it an ideal alternative for budget travelers.

Boutique Riads & Guesthouses

Staying at Tangier's boutique riads or guesthouses provides a more intimate and genuine Moroccan experience. These lovely motels frequently include classic architecture, individualized service, and a comfortable setting.

Dar Jameel: This beautifully renovated riad in the medina provides a serene getaway with finely appointed rooms and a peaceful garden. The rooftop patio offers panoramic views of the city and the sea, making it the ideal place to unwind after a day of exploration.

Riad Arous Chamel: Situated in the center of the medina, Riad Arous Chamel features individually furnished rooms, a lovely courtyard, and a rooftop terrace with breathtaking views. The cheerful hosts greet you warmly and give individual service, ensuring that your stay is unforgettable.

Dar Sultan: This boutique guesthouse blends traditional Moroccan design with contemporary amenities. Dar Sultan, located in the Kasbah, features nicely designed rooms, a verdant garden, and a rooftop terrace with stunning views of the Strait of Gibraltar.

Unique Stays & Airbnbs
Tangier has a variety of unique stays and Airbnb accommodations for guests looking for something out of the ordinary. From contemporary apartments with sea views to eccentric lodgings in the medina, each choice offers a unique and unforgettable experience.

Modern Apartment with Sea View: Located on the Corniche, this trendy Airbnb provides contemporary design, amazing sea views, and all of the comforts of home. Its handy position between the beach and city center gives it an excellent starting point for exploring Tangier.

Traditional Medina House: Stay in a traditional Moroccan house to experience the charm of Tangier's medina. Beautiful tiles, exquisite woodwork, and quiet courtyards are common features of these Airbnbs, creating a genuine and one-of-a-kind experience.

Eco-Friendly Retreat: If you want to get away from the noise and bustle of the city, try an eco-friendly refuge on the outskirts of Tangier. These lodgings provide sustainable living with contemporary comforts surrounded by nature's splendor.

Finally, Tangier has a diverse range of hotel alternatives to meet any traveler's preferences and budget. Tangier's hospitality scene provides a remarkable and pleasant experience, whether you desire the grandeur of luxury hotels, the beauty of boutique riads, or the affordability of low-cost accommodations. So, pick your ideal home away from home and prepare to discover the wonderful city of Tangier.

Must-See Attractions

Tangier is a city full of history, culture, and breathtaking scenery. Its unique location at a crossroads of civilizations has endowed it with a rich tapestry of attractions, each conveying a narrative about the city's lively history and dynamic present. From historic strongholds to lively marketplaces and magnificent natural surroundings, Tangier has a wealth of must-see sites that will captivate you. Let's look at the highlights that make this city a particularly intriguing destination.

The Kasbah Museum

The Kasbah Museum, situated in the old Dar el Makhzen castle and perched atop the medina's highest point, is a cultural jewel in Tangier. This museum provides an intriguing tour through the region's history, displaying relics from ancient periods to the present. The palace, which was erected in the 17th century, is a Moroccan architectural masterpiece, complete with beautiful tilework, huge courtyards, and lush gardens.

Inside, you'll discover a remarkable collection of archeological treasures, including Roman mosaics,

Phoenician antiquities, and Islamic art. The museum also emphasizes Tangier's history as a cultural melting pot, with exhibitions dedicated to the city's Jewish, Christian, and Muslim inhabitants. As you explore the museum, you will obtain a better knowledge of Tangier's historical significance and cultural richness.

The American Legation Museum

The American Legation Museum is the only U.S. institution in Tangier, demonstrating the city's global links. National Historic Landmark situated outside of the United States. This museum, located in a lovely 19th-century edifice in the medina, honors Morocco's long-standing diplomatic links with the United States.

The museum's displays showcase the rich history of Moroccan-American connections, with documents, images, and artworks depicting this unique link. One of the museum's most prominent items is the "Paul Bowles Wing," which honors the American writer and composer who made Tangier his home. The museum also offers temporary exhibitions, cultural events, and educational activities, making it a vibrant cultural center in the heart of the medina.

The Medina of Tangier

Tangier's medina is a tangle of small alleyways, busy marketplaces, and old buildings. Exploring the medina is an experience unto itself, with each turn revealing something new and exciting. This old district is a living witness to Tangier's rich past, where traditional Moroccan life still thrives.

As you travel around the medina, you'll come across bustling souks offering everything from spices and fabrics to jewelry and pottery. The Grand Mosque, with its unique tower, is a prominent point, while the Petit Socco plaza is ideal for relaxing and people-watching from a café patio. Don't miss the chance to see some of the medina's antique riads, many of which have been turned into delightful guesthouses and boutique hotels.

The medina's attraction stems from its authenticity and ability to transport you back in time. Whether you're looking for souvenirs, discovering secret courtyards, or simply taking in the ambiance, the medina is a must-see destination that encapsulates the spirit of Tangier.

The Grand Socco

The Grand Socco, also known as Place du 9 Avril 1947, is a lively area that serves as the entrance to the medina. This colorful plaza is a hive of activity where both residents and tourists gather to chat, shop, and enjoy the vibrant street life.

The area is flanked by ancient structures, notably the Cinéma Rif, a magnificently restored movie theater that currently functions as a cultural center and café. The Grand Socco also hosts a daily market where sellers offer fresh food, flowers, and a variety of merchandise. It's an excellent spot to soak up the local culture while watching the rush and bustle of daily life in Tangier.

A monument of the late King Mohammed V sits in the center of the square, honoring his important speech in 1947 that represented a watershed moment in Morocco's quest for independence. The Grand Socco is more than simply a historical relic; it is a bustling area where the past and present meet, providing a peek into Tangier's spirit.

Cape Spartel

Cape Spartel is a must-see destination for magnificent natural beauty and panoramic vistas. This magnificent promontory, located approximately 14 kilometers west of Tangier, represents the point at where the Mediterranean Sea meets the Atlantic Ocean. The cape is home to a magnificent lighthouse established by the Sultan of Morocco in 1864, which continues to guide ships over the dangerous waters of the Strait of Gibraltar.

Cape Spartel provides breathtaking views of the jagged coastline and huge expanse of the Atlantic. On clear days, you can see Spain's southern coast across the strait. The region surrounding the coast is ideal for hiking and picnics, with various routes winding through beautiful pine trees and providing breathtaking views.

One of the attractions in Cape Spartel is the adjacent Hercules Cave, a natural wonder steeped in legend. According to tradition, the Greek hero Hercules slept here amid his labors. The cave has an outstanding aperture fashioned like the continent of Africa, which creates a dramatic silhouette against the sea. It's a popular picture location and provides an interesting peek into the region's geological past.

In summary, Tangier's must-see sites provide a riveting combination of history, culture, and natural beauty. From the ancient treasures of the Kasbah Museum and the American Legation Museum to the bustling charm of the medina and the Grand Socco, as well as the breathtaking views of Cape Spartel, these attractions capture the soul of this dynamic city. Tangier offers a variety of activities that will amaze and inspire you, whether you are a history buff, a cultural enthusiast, or a nature lover.

Discovering Tangiers' Hidden Gems

Beyond its well-known sites, Tangier is a city full of hidden jewels waiting to be found. These off-the-beaten-path sites provide a better understanding of the city's history, culture, and natural beauty. Tangier's hidden gems, which range from quiet parks and ancient caverns to historic cathedrals and breathtaking lighthouses, provide one-of-a-kind experiences that will enhance your vacation. Let's have a look at some of these fascinating places that are off the beaten path.

Perdicaris Park

Perdicaris Park, also known as Parc Perdicaris or Rmilat, is a lush oasis on Tangier's outskirts that provides a calm respite from the city's hustle and bustle. This large park is named for Ion Perdicaris, an American-Greek ambassador and rich businessman who originally owned the estate. The park's history is intriguing, with stories of Perdicaris' capture by Moroccan tribesmen in 1904, which sparked worldwide diplomatic talks.

Perdicaris Park is a popular destination for both locals and visitors, with lush woodlands, meandering pathways, and stunning overlooks. The park's rich flora and wildlife make it an ideal location for nature walks, bird viewing, and picnicking. As you walk the well-kept roads, you'll come across gorgeous locations facing the Mediterranean Sea, with amazing vistas, especially after sunset. Perdicaris Park is an excellent choice for individuals seeking quiet and natural beauty in Tangier.

Caves of Hercules

The Caves of Hercules are one of Tangier's most intriguing natural attractions, steeped in myth and tradition. These ancient caves, located around 14 kilometers west of the city at Cape Spartel, are said to have served as a resting area for the Greek hero Hercules during his labors. The caverns are notable for its remarkable entrance, which is fashioned like the continent of Africa and provides a spectacular view of the Atlantic Ocean.

Visitors may explore the enormous cave system, which includes natural and man-made chambers. Throughout history, the caverns have served a variety of uses, including as a millstone quarry and a pirate haven. Inside, you'll find unique rock formations and a feeling of mystery that will captivate your mind. The Caves of Hercules, with its natural beauty and mythical legends, are a must-see hidden gem in Tangier.

Saint Andrew's Church

St. Andrew's Church is a unique and lovely location that symbolizes Tangier's varied background. This Anglican church, erected in 1894, combines Gothic and Moorish architectural elements, making it a notable landmark in the city. St. Andrew's Church, which is near the Grand Socco, is noteworthy for its whitewashed walls and exquisite architecture.

Inside, the chapel has stunning stained-glass windows and elaborate woodwork sculptures. One of the most prominent features is the Lord's Prayer, which is etched in Arabic above the altar and represents Tangier's healthy coexistence of various cultures and religions. The church's beautiful garden and well-kept cemetery, where renowned expatriates are buried, contribute to the peaceful ambiance.

St. Andrew's Church continues to serve both the local and expat populations by organizing regular services and cultural activities. It provides a calm refuge as well as a view into Tangier's rich history and spirituality.

Tangier Cemetery

The Tangier Cemetery, also known as the Christian Cemetery, is a tranquil and introspective spot that serves as a sad reflection of the city's cosmopolitan heritage. This cemetery, located near the medina, serves as the final resting place for many foreigners who lived and died in Tangier, including diplomats, merchants, and explorers.

The cemetery is immaculately kept, with shaded walks, blooming flowers, and old gravestones that recount the tales of the people who helped shape Tangier's unique cultural tapestry. Among the prominent graves are those of American writer Paul Bowles and his wife Jane Bowles, both of whom played important roles in Tangier's literary scene.

A visit to Tangier Cemetery is a quiet experience, providing a moment of calm and thought amidst the city's lively vitality. It is a location where history and memory intersect, allowing visitors to pay their respects and connect with Tangier's rich legacy.

The Phare de Tanger (Lighthouse of Tangier)

The Phare de Tanger, often known as the Tangier Lighthouse, is a stunning landmark with panoramic views of the city and surrounding shoreline. This ancient lighthouse, located on the northern extremity of the medina near the entrance to the harbor, has directed ships over the Strait of Gibraltar since the late nineteenth century.

The lighthouse's white tower, towering tall against the turquoise backdrop of the sea, is a memorable sight. Visitors may climb to the summit for a stunning view of the bustling harbor, distant hills of Spain, and Tangier's enormous cityscape. The area surrounding the lighthouse is ideal for a leisurely stroll, with various vistas and seats to rest and enjoy the sight.

The Phare de Tanger is not only a practical beacon for marine navigation, but it also represents Tangier's long-standing relationship to the sea. Its tranquil setting and breathtaking vistas make it a hidden treasure that provides a unique perspective on the city's attractiveness.

Finally, Tangier's hidden treasures provide a variety of experiences outside the typical tourist sites. These lesser-known places, from the quiet beauty of Perdicaris Park and the fabled appeal of the Caves of Hercules to the cosmopolitan charm of St. Andrew's Church and the reflected tranquility of Tangier Cemetery, provide a deeper connection to the city's rich history and culture. The Phare de

Tanger offers a picturesque highlight to your journey, displaying Tangier's lasting maritime heritage. As you discover these hidden gems, you'll have a better understanding of Tangier's eclectic and intriguing character.

Cultural Experiences

Tangier is a city where history, culture, and tradition all mingle together to create a lively and dynamic environment. Participating in the city's many cultural activities is one of the finest ways to properly appreciate its charm. Tangier has several options to immerse oneself in its distinct past, including participation in traditional rites and exploration of local art. Here are some cultural activities to make your trip to Tangier unique.

Traditional Moroccan Tea Ceremony

The traditional Moroccan tea ceremony is an essential component of the country's social and cultural fabric. Mint tea, sometimes known as "Moroccan whiskey," symbolizes hospitality and camaraderie. Participating in a tea ceremony is a lovely opportunity to have direct familiarity with Moroccan culture.

Typically, the ritual consists of boiling green tea with fresh mint leaves and a substantial amount of sugar. The leader of the home normally prepares the tea, which is served in gorgeous, decorative teapots and cups. The method of pouring tea is an art form in and of itself; the tea is poured from a height to produce a frothy top, which is said to improve the flavor.

Many local tea cafes, or "salons de thé," provide guests with the opportunity to enjoy this experience. Several cultural institutes and guided tours also provide tea ceremonies, where you may learn about the ritual's significance while also enjoying the subtle aromas of Moroccan mint tea in an authentic atmosphere.

Henna Arts & Workshops

Henna art is a lovely and traditional kind of body adornment in Morocco, commonly utilized for festivities and special events. The complex patterns, which are often done to the hands and feet, have deep cultural and symbolic connotations. Participating in a henna workshop provides a fresh perspective on this ancient art form.

Many local artists and cultural institutes in Tangier host henna classes where you may learn about the history and methods of henna application. These courses provide hands-on experiences in which you may make your own designs with the aid of expert henna artists. It's an excellent opportunity to learn about the cultural significance of henna while also producing a lasting memory of your trip.

For those who wish to enjoy henna art without attending a course, there are various talented artists throughout the medina who can create stunning henna patterns for you. It's a great way to appreciate Moroccan culture and bring a bit of it with you on your travels.

Moroccan Culinary Classes

Moroccan cuisine is well-known for its complex tastes, fragrant spices, and numerous influences. Taking a cooking class in Tangier is a great opportunity to learn about the country's culinary traditions and how to produce some of its most popular meals.

Many culinary schools and local chefs provide workshops to teach you how to create classic Moroccan meals like tagine, couscous, and pastilla. These sessions frequently begin with a trip to a local market, where you may choose fresh products and learn about the spices and herbs that are essential to Moroccan cuisine.

During the workshop, you'll receive hands-on experience cooking the meals, taught by skilled chefs who will reveal their culinary secrets and skills. The sessions generally end with a shared supper where you can enjoy the benefits of your effort and sample the delectable flavors of Moroccan cuisine. It's an excellent opportunity to deepen your passion for Moroccan cuisine while also learning new skills to wow your friends and family.

Local Music & Dance Performances

Music and dance are integral parts of Moroccan culture, with a wide range of genres and customs reflecting the country's unique background. Local music and dance performances in Tangier provide a lively and fascinating peek into Moroccan culture.

Tangier has various locations where you may see live performances of traditional Moroccan music such as Andalusian, Gnawa, and Chaabi. Andalusian music, which originated in medieval Spain, has complicated melodies and rhythms that are frequently accompanied by literary lyrics. Gnawa music, known for its hypnotic rhythms and spiritual themes, developed in sub-Saharan African communities in Morocco. Chaabi, or "popular" music, is a vibrant genre that combines many regional traditions and is frequently performed at festivities and festivals.

Tangier's cultural institutions, cafés, and concert halls present frequent performances featuring these intriguing musical traditions. Local festivals and gatherings sometimes include music and dance, creating a holistic cultural experience.

Art Gallery & Exhibitions

Tangier has long served as a source of inspiration for international artists, authors, and creatives. The city's robust art scene reflects its rich cultural legacy and role as a crossroads of civilizations. Exploring Tangier's art galleries and exhibitions is an excellent opportunity to interact with the city's artistic energy and learn about the works of local and international artists.

Several well-known art galleries in Tangier display a wide spectrum of modern and traditional Moroccan art. The Galerie Delacroix, named after the famed French painter Eugène Delacroix, who visited Tangier in the nineteenth century, is one of the city's most notable galleries. It showcases alternating exhibits of paintings, sculptures, and photographs that showcase Moroccan artists' ability and inventiveness.

Another famous gallery is the Loft Art Gallery, which exhibits modern Moroccan and African art and provides a forum for both young and experienced artists to showcase their work. The

Tangier American Legation Museum also conducts art exhibitions that commemorate cultural interchange between Morocco and the United States.

Tangier offers a number of art festivals and cultural events throughout the year, including the Tangier International Film Festival and the Jazz Festival, all of which feature art exhibitions and concerts. These events offer an exciting and interactive approach to explore the city's creative vitality.

Finally, Tangier provides a variety of cultural events that allow tourists to immerse themselves in the city's rich legacy and customs. Whether you're sipping mint tea in a traditional ceremony, learning how to apply henna patterns, mastering the art of Moroccan cuisine, experiencing live music and dancing, or visiting local art galleries, these activities let you connect with Tangier's distinct cultural tapestry. Take advantage of these possibilities to interact with the local culture and make lasting memories of your stay in this wonderful city.

Day Trips & Excursions

While Tangier itself has a plethora of activities and experiences, the surrounding areas also have amazing places that are ideal for day trips and excursions. From attractive seaside towns and ancient cities to magnificent natural settings, there is a lot to see around Tangier. Here are some of the most exciting day trip possibilities to enhance your Moroccan journey.

Asilah: Art and Coastal Beauty

Asilah, located only a short drive south of Tangier, is a beautiful beach town famed for its gorgeous whitewashed houses, bright paintings, and relaxed attitude. The town has a long history reaching back to the Phoenician period, but now it is known as an artistic sanctuary.

Walking through Asilah's medina, you will be charmed by the vibrant street art on the walls. Each summer, the town organizes the Asilah Arts Festival, which brings artists from all over the world to paint new murals, perform, and display their work. The event transforms Asilah into an open-air gallery, giving it a busy and exciting location to visit.

Aside from its artistic attraction, Asilah has wonderful beaches where you may relax and enjoy the sun. The neighboring Paradise Beach, with its golden beaches and crystal blue seas, is ideal for swimming and picnics. Asilah's peaceful atmosphere, along with its cultural and natural beauties, make it an excellent day trip destination.

Tetouan: A UNESCO World Heritage Site

Tetouan, located about 60 kilometers southeast of Tangier, is a historically and culturally rich city. Its medina is a UNESCO World Heritage Site known for its well-preserved architecture and traditional Moroccan culture.

Tetouan's medina is a maze of small alleyways, thriving marketplaces, and old structures. Unlike Tangier's more cosmopolitan medina, Tetouan's old town has a unique traditional character, providing a look into the past. Visit the Royal Palace, the Ethnographic Museum, and the School of Arts and Crafts to see artists at work.

Andalusian influence may be seen in the city's architecture, food, and cultural customs, owing to the arrival of Andalusian exiles in the 15th century. Tetouan also has a strong artistic sector, with several galleries and cultural institutions showing Moroccan and Andalusian artwork.

A visit to Tetouan provides a comprehensive cultural experience, combining history, art, and traditional Moroccan life in an authentic and timeless environment.

Chefchaouen: The Blue City

Chefchaouen, often known as the "Blue City" or "Blue Pearl," is one of Morocco's most gorgeous towns. Chefchaouen, located in the Rif Mountains and roughly two hours from Tangier, is well-known for its beautiful blue-painted streets and houses.

The town's distinct color palette creates a surreal ambiance, making it a popular choice for photographers and vacationers looking for a peaceful retreat. As you go through the medina's twisting lanes, you will come across delightful stores selling local crafts, fabrics, and artisanal products. The Plaza Uta el-Hammam, the center plaza, is a fantastic location to unwind with a mint tea and watch the world go by.

In addition to its aesthetic appeal, Chefchaouen provides a plethora of outdoor sports. The nearby Rif Mountains are suitable for trekking, with routes leading to picturesque overlooks and waterfalls, including the famed Akchour Waterfalls. Whether you are visiting the town or getting out into nature, Chefchaouen offers a peaceful and intriguing experience.

Rif Mountains: Hiking and Nature

For nature lovers and adventure seekers, the Rif Mountains provide a rough and magnificent scenery ideal for climbing, trekking, and exploration. This mountain range spans northern Morocco and offers several chances for outdoor activity.

Talassemtane National Park, in Chefchaouen, is one of the Rif Mountains' most popular hiking sites. The park is home to a rich range of vegetation and animals, including some indigenous species. Hiking routes in the park take you through lush woods, steep valleys, and up to breathtaking overlooks with panoramic views of the surrounding countryside.

Another popular site in the Rif Mountains is Jebel Kelti, a summit with hard walks and wonderful vistas. The region's natural beauty and calm give a welcome contrast to the bustling cities and towns, making it a wonderful choice for a day of outdoor exploration.

Laroche: Archaeological Ruins & Beaches

Larache, located on the Atlantic coast around 90 kilometers south of Tangier, is a medieval town that mixes archeological fascination with coastal attractiveness. The town's strategic location has made it a popular colony for many civilizations, including the Phoenicians, Romans, and Moors.

One of Laroche's most notable attractions is the adjacent ancient site of Lixus. This historic city, which dates back to the Phoenician period, provides an intriguing look into Morocco's early past. Visitors may wander among the ruins of temples, spas, and an amphitheater, all situated against the backdrop of the Loukkos River.

In addition to its historical significance, Larache has lovely beaches where you may unwind and enjoy the water. The town's primary beach, Playa de Rmilat, is popular for sunbathing and swimming, while the quieter beaches to the north provide a more private environment.

Laroche's combination of history, culture, and natural beauty makes it a worthwhile day excursion from Tangier, offering both educational and recreational opportunities.

In conclusion, Tangier's neighboring areas provide a wide range of day trips and excursions to suit a variety of interests, including art and history, nature, and leisure. Whether you are exploring the beautiful lanes of Asilah, delving into Tetouan's cultural legacy, roaming the blue alleys of Chefchaouen, climbing in the Rif Mountains, or discovering ancient ruins in Larache, each site offers a new depth to your Moroccan journey. These excursions not only help you comprehend the country's rich history, but they also give remarkable experiences to supplement your time in Tangier.

Shopping in Tangiers

Tangier shopping is an adventure in and of itself, with a mix of historic markets, trendy shops, and one-of-a-kind items that encapsulate Moroccan culture. Tangier has something for everyone, from busy souks full of brilliant colors and tantalizing fragrances to stylish stores presenting trendy fashion. Here's a guide to navigating the city's numerous shopping options.

Souks and Market

Tangier's retail environment revolves around its souks and markets, where you can immerse yourself in local culture while discovering a wide range of items. The Grand Socco (Socco Grande) is a busy market plaza that serves as the entrance to the old medina. The vendors here sell everything from fresh food and spices to homemade crafts and fabrics.

Moving deeper into the medina, the Petit Socco (Socco Chico) is another bustling market district where you may peruse a variety of stores and booths. The tight, meandering lanes are crowded with sellers selling traditional Moroccan items including carpets, ceramics, lanterns, and leather goods. The bustling ambiance, along with the market's noises and fragrances, creates an amazing shopping experience.

The souks are also an excellent source for unusual souvenirs and presents. If you are seeking for handcrafted carpets, delicate jewelry, or aromatic spices, Tangier's marketplaces provide plenty of possibilities. Remember to spend your time investigating, as some of the finest treasures are typically buried in the market's quieter areas.

Moroccan Handicrafts & Souvenirs

Moroccan handicrafts are known for their high quality and skill, and Tangier is no exception when it comes to stunning handcrafted items. The city is home to several stores and ateliers where you may buy stunning handcrafted products that make ideal souvenirs or presents.

Traditional Berber rugs are one of Morocco's most popular handicrafts. These carpets are recognized for their complex designs and brilliant colors, with each expressing a narrative about the location and the weaver. Many businesses in the medina and across the city specialize in these carpets, providing a variety of designs and sizes.

Moroccan ceramics is another must-buy item. Fez's characteristic blue and white pottery are particularly popular, but there are many more types and colors available. These finely created pieces, which range from plates and bowls to vases and tiles, are excellent decorative items.

Leather items are another example of Moroccan workmanship. Tangier's leather markets sell a variety of items, including purses, wallets, belts, and slippers (babouches). The quality of Moroccan leather is superb, making these goods both durable and fashionable.

Other popular souvenirs include traditional Moroccan lamps with complex metalwork and colorful glass, hand-painted tiles, jewelry, and traditional clothes like djellabas and kaftans.

Antique Stores & Boutiques

Tangier's antique stores and boutiques are a treasure trove of fascinating items for people who appreciate the distinctive and historical. These shops frequently sell a combination of Moroccan antiques, vintage products, and one-of-a-kind objects that represent the city's rich cultural background.

Antique stores in Tangier often sell a wide range of objects, including antique coins, furniture, textiles, and relics from various times in the city's history. Browsing these boutiques is like going back in time, with each item conveying a narrative about Tangier's history.

Boutiques, on the other hand, provide a more contemporary shopping experience by combining traditional Moroccan aesthetics with modern design. Many of these boutiques are located in Tangier's more expensive areas, such as the Martian and the New Town. A carefully chosen assortment of clothes, accessories, home décor, and art is available here, with many pieces produced by local designers and craftsmen.

Shopping at these stores allows you to explore the unique side of Moroccan design, where heritage and modernity intersect in new and stylish ways.

Contemporary Fashion & Design

Tangier is more than simply traditional crafts; it also has a vibrant modern fashion and design sector. The city's international culture is mirrored in its fashion boutiques and design shops, which provide contemporary and trendy things to suit current tastes.

Many local designers are inspired by Morocco's rich cultural past and incorporate traditional aspects into contemporary fashion. This confluence produces distinctive apparel and accessories that combine the old and new. Tangier's fashion stores offer something for everyone, whether you are seeking for sophisticated clothing, distinctive jewelry, or trendy accessories.

Contemporary Moroccan design may be found in both clothes and home decor. Several stores specialize in modern furniture, lighting, and decorative items with traditional Moroccan designs and materials. These pieces give a sense of Moroccan beauty to any house, making them ideal for anyone wishing to bring a bit of Tangier home with them.

Tips for Bargaining

Bargaining is a prevalent activity in Morocco, particularly in the souks and markets, and it is a necessary skill for obtaining the best prices. Here are some suggestions to help you negotiate the negotiation process like an expert:

Do Your Research: Before going to the markets, figure out what you want to buy and what the normal pricing is for those things. This will provide you with a starting point and assist you in determining a reasonable price.

Start Low: When negotiations, make a lower offer than you are willing to pay. This allows you to bargain and obtain a price that both you and the vendor are satisfied with.

Be Polite and Friendly: Building rapport is just as important as negotiating a price. Being kind and nice might go a long way toward establishing a favorable rapport with the vendor.

Do not Show Too Much Enthusiasm: If you express too much interest in an item, the seller may be less ready to negotiate the price. Keep your excitement in check until the negotiations are completed.

Be Prepared to Walk Away: If the price is not right, be ready to walk away. Frequently, vendors will call you back with a higher offer. If not, there are typically other vendors selling comparable products.

Know When to Stop: When you have reached a price you believe is reasonable, accept it politely.

Over Bargaining can be perceived as rude and may sour the conversation.

In conclusion, shopping in Tangier is a pleasant experience that combines traditional marketplaces, handcrafted products, one-of-a-kind antiques, and modern fashion. Tangier's diversified retail culture offers something for everyone, whether you are looking for a handmade rug, Moroccan ceramics, a fashionable suit, or an antique gem. Embrace the vivid energy of the souks, browse the lovely boutiques, and remember to negotiate to make the most of your shopping trip in this interesting city.

Culinary Delights of Tangier

Tangier is a city that combines culinary traditions from around Morocco and beyond, providing a rich and diverse gourmet experience. Tangier's culinary environment offers something for everyone's taste, from traditional Moroccan meals to contemporary fine dining, street food to seafood feasts. Here's a guide to the delectable treats available in this dynamic city.

Traditional Moroccan Cuisine

Traditional Moroccan food is a sensory delight, with powerful tastes, fragrant spices, and rich ingredients. When in Tangier, you must try these iconic meals.

Tagine: Named after the earthenware pot in which it is prepared, is a slow-cooked stew made with meat (usually chicken, lamb, or beef), vegetables, and a spice combination that includes cumin, coriander, and cinnamon. Each tagine is unique, and they are frequently decorated with olives, preserved lemons, and dried fruits.

Couscous: This popular Moroccan dish consists of steaming semolina grains topped with a variety of vegetables and meat, sometimes served with a delicious broth. Friday is usually Couscous Day in Morocco, and many restaurants in Tangier serve it as a special.

Harira: This substantial soup, commonly eaten during Ramadan, is prepared with tomatoes, lentils, chickpeas, and a variety of spices. It is commonly served with dates and chebakia, which are honey-drenched pastries.

Pastilla: A savory-sweet pastry made with spiced pigeon or chicken, almonds, and cinnamon, wrapped in thin layers of phyllo dough and coated with powdered sugar.

Tangier's small diners and traditional Moroccan restaurants provide these delicacies, which have been passed down through generations, maintaining the region's unique culinary history.

Street Food & Snacks

Tangier's street food culture provides a more relaxed and engaging eating experience, with a variety of tasty snacks and short eats. Exploring the street sellers and food booths is a unique journey that reveals the city's lively culinary culture.

Bissara is a thick, soothing soup cooked with dried fava beans and seasoned with olive oil, cumin, and paprika. It is typically served with warm bread and provides a filling breakfast or snack.

Maakouda: Garlic, cumin, and parsley season these delicious potato fritters, which are crunchy on the exterior and tender on the inside. They are often offered by street sellers and make an excellent fast and tasty snack.

Sfenj: Moroccan doughnuts known as sfenj are a popular delicacy, sometimes served with a cup of mint tea. These airy, somewhat chewy doughnuts are cooked to golden perfection and available at numerous street vendors.

Kebabs: Another popular street snack is grilled meat skewers, known as brochettes. Whether it is delicious lamb, chicken, or beef, these kebabs are frequently marinated in spices and cooked over open flames, resulting in a savory and fulfilling snack.

Msemmen: A flaky and buttery Moroccan pancake that is commonly eaten with honey or cheese. Street sellers cook them fresh, making them an excellent morning or lunchtime snack.

Fine-Dining Restaurants

Tangier's eating scene also includes a number of fine dining establishments with sophisticated cuisine and gorgeous surroundings. These venues frequently combine traditional Moroccan flavors with modern culinary methods, resulting in a distinctive and upmarket eating experience.

El Morocco Club: Located in Kasbah, El Morocco Club is well-known for its stylish environment and excellent Moroccan food. The cuisine combines local ingredients with foreign influences, resulting in unique meals that please the palette.

La Fabrique: This trendy restaurant specializes in Mediterranean and Moroccan food. The chef's innovative approach and the restaurant's elegant design make it a popular choice for a memorable night out.

Dar Nour: Located in a lovely riad, Dar Nour offers a friendly, intimate ambiance with a menu that emphasizes Moroccan and Mediterranean tastes. The rooftop patio provides excellent views of the city, which enhances the eating experience.

Restaurant Saveur de Poisson: Known for its fresh fish and unusual cooking methods, this restaurant offers a set menu with a range of seafood dishes. The small environment and rustic charm contribute to its allure.

These fine dining alternatives offer the opportunity to appreciate great food in attractively designed settings, making each meal an unforgettable experience.

Vegetarian & Vegan Options

Tangier's culinary culture also caters to vegetarians and vegans, with numerous eateries providing plant-based alternatives that do not sacrifice flavor or diversity.

Vegetarian Tagine: Many traditional Moroccan restaurants provide vegetarian tagines that include seasonal vegetables, chickpeas, and fragrant spices. These recipes are substantial and fulfilling, demonstrating the diversity of Moroccan cuisine.

Salads and Mezze: Moroccan cuisine has a range of fresh salads and mezze, including zaalouk (smoked eggplant salad), taktouka (pepper and tomato salad), and lentil salad. These recipes are generally served with warm bread and make for a nutritious and pleasant supper.

Café Hafa: This traditional café serves a variety of vegetarian snacks and small meals, as well as its signature mint tea. The café's cliffside location offers breathtaking views of the Strait of Gibraltar, making it a popular destination for both residents and visitors.

Pure Food: A modern cafe that focuses on health-conscious and plant-based food. The menu includes fresh salads, smoothies, and vegan-friendly options. It is an excellent spot to eat a healthy and delectable dinner in a modern atmosphere.

With a growing awareness of dietary concerns, more Tangier restaurants are broadening their menus to offer vegetarian and vegan alternatives, ensuring that all tourists may sample the city's gastronomic pleasures.

Best Places for Seafood

Given Tangier's seaside position, it is not surprising that the city serves some of Morocco's freshest and most flavorful seafood. Here are some of the best places to eat a seafood feast.

Restaurant Populaire Saveur de Poisson: This hidden treasure is well-known for its seafood cuisine, which changes daily depending on the catch of the day. The modest location and distinctive culinary technique make it a must-see for seafood enthusiasts.

Restaurant La Merveille: Located near the harbor, La Merveille specializes in fresh seafood dishes such as grilled fish and seafood paella. The restaurant's relaxed ambiance and coastal views enhance its appeal.

Le Saveur du Poisson: Another wonderful seafood option, Le Saveur du Poisson serves a set menu including a selection of fish and shellfish served with traditional Moroccan spices and herbs. The rustic, warm environment creates a great eating experience.

Rif Kebdani: Located in the medina, Rif Kebdani is famous for its seafood tagines and grilled fish. The restaurant's pleasant service and genuine cuisine have gained it a devoted following from both residents and visitors.

These seafood restaurants offer the opportunity to taste the ocean's abundance while using Moroccan cuisine's distinct flavors and methods.

In conclusion, Tangier's culinary scene is as diverse and dynamic as the city itself. Tangier provides a diverse and gratifying culinary adventure, whether you are indulging in traditional Moroccan delicacies, discovering the lively street food scene, dining at a nice restaurant, or looking for vegetarian or vegan choices. The city's beachfront setting also assures that seafood lovers will find plenty to satisfy their palates. Accept the tastes of Tangier and make its gastronomic pleasures a highlight of your Moroccan journey.

Nightlife & Entertainment

Tangier develops into a thriving nightlife and entertainment destination once the sun sets. Tangier has a broad range of nocturnal activities to suit every taste, whether you want to spend a classy evening at a fashionable bar, immerse yourself in traditional Moroccan music, dance the night away at a club, or attend a cultural event. Let us explore the vibrant nightlife scene of this wonderful city.

Trendy Bars & Lounges

Tangier's bar and lounge culture is as diverse as the city, combining modern refinement with a touch of Moroccan charm. Here are some must-see destinations for an evening of fashionable relaxation:

Sky 17: Situated atop the El Minzah Hotel, Sky 17 provides magnificent views of the city and the Mediterranean Sea. This stylish rooftop bar is ideal for drinking drinks and watching the sunset or stargazing at night. The classy environment and large drink selection make it popular among both residents and visitors.

Le Mirage: Located along the shore, Le Mirage offers beautiful ocean views and a relaxed ambiance. The bar's outside patio is a great place to relax with a drink, listen to live music, and take in the sea breeze.

La Bodega: Known for its boisterous ambiance and quirky décor, provides a dynamic backdrop for an evening out. The bar offers a wide selection of drinks, wines, and tapas, making it an excellent spot to begin your night.

Cinco Lounge: This contemporary lounge club is known for its attractive decor and inventive drinks. Cinco Lounge, located in the center of Tangier, is a popular destination for people wishing to spend a nice night out with friends.

Traditional Moroccan Music Venues

For a real cultural experience, visit Tangier's traditional Moroccan music venues. These venues provide an insight into Morocco's rich musical tradition via captivating and enchanting performances.

Club El Morocco: Located in the Kasbah, Club El Morocco is a historic location where you can hear live performances of traditional Moroccan music such as Gnawa and Andalusian genres. The compact environment and authentic ambiance make it a one-of-a-kind destination for experiencing Morocco's deep melodies.

Dar Baroud: This cultural center has regular performances of traditional Moroccan music, dance, and poetry. The magnificently furnished auditorium, with its complex mosaics and brilliant colors, makes an excellent setting for an evening of cultural immersion.

Café Hafa: Although more known for its picturesque vistas and mint tea, Café Hafa occasionally hosts live performances of traditional Moroccan music. The café's relaxing environment and cliffside position make it ideal for experiencing Tangier's rhythms.

Nightclubs & Dance Areas

Tangier's nightlife would be incomplete without its selection of nightclubs and dance clubs, where you can let free and dance till the early hours of the morning.

Tangerinn is a renowned nightclub in the city center that is noted for its vibrant atmosphere, live DJ performances, and large dance floor. The club draws a mix of locals and visitors, resulting in a vibrant and diverse atmosphere.

Bora Bora: This seaside club provides a one-of-a-kind party experience with its open-air dance floor, tropical ambiance, and breathtaking views of the Mediterranean. Bora Bora has themed evenings and live acts, making it a popular destination for a fun and unforgettable night out.

Discothèque 555: One of Tangier's most well-known nightclubs, Discothèque 555 is the place to go for a night of dancing and entertainment. The club has cutting-edge sound and lighting systems, renowned worldwide DJs, and a lively party environment.

Cultural Performances & Theaters

Tangier's theaters and cultural institutions provide a range of shows that exhibit the city's creative ability.

Gran Teatro Cervantes: This ancient theater, built in 1913, is an architectural treasure and cultural icon in Tangier. Despite being under renovation, the theater has held a number of performances, including plays, concerts, and operas. Keep a look out for the reopening and upcoming activities.

Tangier American Legation Museum: In addition to its unique displays, the Tangier American Legation Museum often offers cultural events such as concerts, seminars, and art exhibitions. The museum's unusual location and rich history make it an exceptional spot to scc Tangier's cultural landscape.

Cinematheque de Tanger: The Cinematheque de Tanger, housed in the ancient Cinema Rif, is a cultural center that shows a wide range of films, including Moroccan cinema, foreign classics, and current works. The facility also holds film festivals, seminars, and talks, providing a rich cultural experience.

Casino & Gaming

Tangier features a few casinos that provide an excellent gaming experience, as well as a variety of entertainment opportunities.

Casino Malabata: Located along the seaside, Casino Malabata has a range of gambling alternatives such as slot machines, poker, blackjack, and roulette. The casino also has live entertainment, a bar, and a restaurant, making it a complete location for a night of fun and excitement.

Casino de Tanger: Located inside the Movenpick Hotel & Casino Malabata Tanger, this casino offers a magnificent gaming experience with a variety of table games, slot machines, and poker. The upmarket atmosphere and excellent service provide a high-end gaming experience.

In conclusion, Tangier's nightlife & entertainment scene are as diverse and vibrant as the city itself. Everyone may find something to enjoy, from contemporary pubs and traditional music venues to nightclubs, theaters, and casinos. Tangier offers an amazing nighttime experience, whether you want to relax with a drink, dance the night away, or take in cultural acts. Accept the city's dynamic nightlife and let it bring a new level of excitement to your Moroccan journey.

Outdoor Activities & Adventures

Tangier's natural beauty and diverse landscapes provide a plethora of outdoor activities and adventures for all types of travelers. Tangier has something fascinating for everyone, whether you enjoy the beach, trek a lot, or are looking for a new trip. Here's a guide to the top outdoor activities in this bustling city.

Beaches & Water Sports

Tangier's coastline has some of Morocco's most stunning beaches, which provide ideal settings for leisure and a variety of water activities.

Achakar Beach: Located west of Tangier, is famed for its magnificent vistas and golden beaches. This beach is ideal for sunbathing, swimming, and beach volleyball. The neighboring Hercules Caves provide historical intrigue to your stay.

Plage Malabata: Located in the Malabata district, this beach provides a calmer ambiance perfect for a family day out. Its tranquil seas are ideal for swimming, and there are various cafés and restaurants along the coast where you can eat with a view.

Plage Merkala: Known for its clean seas and fine dunes, Plage Merkala is popular among both residents and visitors. The beach's good wind conditions make it ideal for windsurfing and kitesurfing.

Water Activities: Tangier's beaches provide good options for water activities including jet skiing, windsurfing, and paddleboarding. Several local providers provide equipment rentals and training for both beginners and expert hobbyists. If you are feeling daring, consider parasailing to enjoy a bird's-eye perspective of the breathtaking coastline.

Hiking Trails & Nature Walks

Tangier has various beautiful routes that exhibit the natural beauty and different landscapes of the area.

Cap Spartel: Just a short drive from the city center, Cap Spartel provides stunning views of the Atlantic Ocean and the Mediterranean Sea. The region has various hiking paths that weave through lush forests and steep cliffs, allowing opportunity to see local species and enjoy the tranquil surroundings.

Perdicaris Park: This ancient park, previously owned by the American Ion Perdicaris, is a lush green paradise ideal for nature hikes. The park's pathways wind through deep trees before opening out to breathtaking views of the sea and city. It is an excellent location for a relaxing trek or a family picnic.

Jebel Moussa: For more experienced hikers, the path to Jebel Moussa, located a little farther from Tangier, is a tough but rewarding climb. The peak offers magnificent views of the Strait of Gibraltar and adjacent regions. The journey takes you through a variety of terrains, including woodlands and rocky outcrops.

Talassemtane National Park: Although it is a bit far from Tangier, this national park in the Rif Mountains is well worth the trek for ardent hikers. The park features a variety of routes that travel through cedar woods, valleys, and waterfalls, providing an immersive nature experience.

Camel & Horseback Riding

Exploring Tangier's scenery on camel or horseback is a one-of-a-kind and fascinating trip.

Camel Rides: A camel ride is a traditional way to move across Tangier's desert-like terrain. Several organizations provide guided camel treks around the beaches and dunes surrounding Cap Spartel and Achakar Beach. It is a pleasant and unique way to take in the beauty while learning about the local culture.

Horseback Riding: Horseback riding is another popular sport in Tangier, offering opportunities for both new and experienced riders. Local stables provide guided trips along the beach, across the countryside, and even into the hills that surround the city. It is a terrific opportunity to interact with nature and breathe fresh air.

Royal Equestrian Club: Located near the city, the Royal Equestrian Club provides horseback riding classes and guided rides for all ability levels. The club's well-trained horses and experienced teachers provide a safe and pleasurable experience.

Golf Courses

Tangier provides tremendous opportunity for golf aficionados to play in gorgeous surroundings.

Royal Country Club: The Royal Country Club of Tangier, established in 1914, is one of Africa's oldest golf courses. The 18-hole course is located against a backdrop of rolling hills and rich foliage, providing a demanding yet picturesque game for players of all skill levels. The club also has a driving range, practice areas, and a clubhouse with food choices.

Tangier Golf Club: Another excellent choice for golfers, the Tangier Golf Club is a well-kept 9-hole course that is ideal for a fast round or for novices wanting to develop their game. The club's welcoming environment and beautiful vistas make it an enjoyable spot to spend the day.

Fishing and Boating

Tangier's seaside position makes it an excellent choice for fishing and boating aficionados.

Fishing Trips: Several local operators provide fishing charters that take you to the greatest fishing sites along the coast. Whether you are a seasoned angler or a beginner, these tours include everything you need for a successful day on the water, including equipment, bait, and expert guides. You may try your hand at capturing several types of fish, such as sea bass, bream, and tuna.

Boating & Sailing: Exploring Tangier's shoreline by boat is an excellent opportunity to experience the city from a new perspective. You may hire a boat or join a guided sailing excursion that will take you along the gorgeous coastline, past historical monuments, and even over the Strait of Gibraltar. Swimming, snorkeling, and dolphin viewing are common activities on these excursions.

Kayaking & Paddleboarding: For a more active trip, hire a kayak or paddleboard and explore the tranquil seas surrounding Tangier. It is a terrific way to go close to the shore, explore secret coves, and work out on the sea.

In conclusion, Tangier's outdoor activities and experiences include something for everyone, from calm beach days and adrenaline-pumping water sports to breathtaking treks and memorable camel rides. Whether you are a nature lover, an adrenaline addict, or someone eager to experience something new, Tangier offers endless options to enjoy the great outdoors and make wonderful memories. Allow the natural beauty and adventurous attitude of this enchanting city to enrich your Moroccan vacation.

Family-Friendly Activities

Tangier provides a variety of family-friendly activities to guarantee that everyone, from the smallest to the elderly, has a great day. Whether you are exploring parks, visiting kid-friendly museums, taking informative tours, or getting up close and personal with animals, there are infinite chances for fun and learning. This is a guide to the top family-friendly activities in Tangier.

Parks & Playgrounds

Tangier's parks and playgrounds are ideal places for families to relax, play, and enjoy the outdoors.

Perdicaris Park: This historical park is ideal for families. It is great for a relaxing family day out, with large open areas, stunning gardens, and several walking pathways. Kids may run and play while their parents have a picnic in the peaceful surroundings. The park's shady spaces and gorgeous views make it an ideal place to spend a sunny afternoon.

Parc de la Ligue Arabe: Located in the center of Tangier, this big urban park is ideal for families seeking a green oasis in the city. The park has well-kept grass, playgrounds, and a diversity of vegetation. Children will enjoy the playgrounds, which provide a variety of equipment for all ages, while parents may rest on seats or wander around the beautiful gardens.

Corniche Gardens: Located along the picturesque coastline route, these gardens provide breathtaking views of the Mediterranean Sea. The green areas and walking routes make it an ideal location for families to take a leisurely walk. The playground grounds are outfitted with sophisticated play structures, guaranteeing that children have a good time.

Child-Friendly Museums

Tangier's museums are entertaining and kid-friendly, so introduce your children to its rich history and culture.

Tangier American Legation Museum: Housed in a historic structure, this one-of-a-kind museum features intriguing displays on Moroccan and American history and relationships. The museum's antiques, pictures, and interactive displays are appealing to youngsters. The attractive courtyards and garden areas offer ample room for children to play and enjoy.

Kasbah Museum: Located in the center of the historic Kasbah, this museum is ideal for family visits. It displays a diverse collection of objects from Morocco's past, including antique pottery, traditional costumes, and beautiful jewelry. The museum's structure is simple to follow, and the displays are engaging for both children and adults. The magnificent environment within the Kasbah walls enhances the experience.

Museum of Contemporary Art: For families with older children who enjoy art, the Museum of Contemporary Art provides a contemporary and stimulating experience. The museum showcases works by Moroccan and international artists, and the exhibits frequently contain interactive and multimedia aspects. It is an excellent venue to foster creativity and engage in debates about art and culture.

Educational Tours & Workshops

Tangier provides a variety of educational excursions and programs that blend learning and enjoyment for the entire family.

Historical Walking Excursions: There are several guided excursions offered that highlight Tangier's rich history and cultural heritage. These tours are designed specifically for families, with fascinating and educational anecdotes about the city's history. Children will love touring the Medina's small alleyways, seeing historical sites, and learning about Tangier's various influences.

Moroccan Cooking Classes: Enroll your family in a Moroccan cooking class to gain hands-on experience. These workshops, which are frequently taught in traditional riads or local kitchens, teach students how to make famous Moroccan meals like tagine, couscous, and pastries. It is a fun and instructive exercise for the whole family, and you get to taste your wonderful creations at the end.

Art & Craft Programs: Many local craftsmen and cultural organizations provide programs for families to learn traditional Moroccan crafts including pottery, weaving, and tile making. These participatory seminars are not only entertaining, but also informative about Morocco's creative past. Children will enjoy the option to design their own mementos.

Zoos & Wildlife Experiences

Tangier and its surroundings provide several possibilities for families to see animals and learn about animal protection.

Tangier Zoo: Located just outside the city, Tangier Zoo is home to a diverse collection of species from throughout the world. The zoo's displays are intended to teach visitors about various animals and environments. Children will enjoy viewing creatures such as lions, zebras, and exotic birds up close. The zoo also provides educational and engaging activities for youngsters.

Jardin Zoologique de Rabat: Although a bit of a drive from Tangier, the Rabat Zoo is well worth the journey for those interested in animals. The zoo has a diverse collection of animals, including Moroccan local species and creatures from other continents. The wide enclosures and informative exhibits provide an instructive and fun experience for people of all ages.

Bird Watching Tours: Tangier's location along migratory pathways makes it an outstanding bird watching destination. Several tour companies provide guided bird watching trips in the surrounding areas, allowing families to observe a variety of bird species in their natural habitats. It is a relaxing & educational activity that nature-loving families will enjoy.

Interactive Exhibits & Entertainment Centres

Tangier has a variety of interactive exhibitions and entertainment facilities for children and families looking for a good time.

Tangier Aquarium: This family-friendly attraction features aquatic life from the Mediterranean Sea and beyond. The aquarium's interactive displays and touch tanks allow youngsters to learn about marine ecosystems while also getting up close to diverse sea animals. Educational activities and feeding sessions enhance the enjoyment.

Fun City Tangier: An indoor entertainment facility, provides a variety of activities for children of all ages. The facility includes play spaces, arcade games, and adventure zones, providing hours of amusement. It is an excellent area to go on a rainy day or when you need a break from touring.

Cinema Rif: Located in the ancient Grand Socco, Cinema Rif is a cultural center that frequently shows family-friendly films and offers special events. The cinema's comfortable environment and broad programming make it an enjoyable visit for families. Check the schedule for children's films, animated movies, and other family-friendly screenings.

In conclusion, Tangier is an excellent family vacation location, with a diverse choice of activities to suit all ages and interests. There are several exciting and fascinating activities to choose from, like touring parks and museums, participating in educational programs, and experiencing animal encounters. Enjoy the opportunity to make unforgettable memories with your family while exploring Tangier's colorful and diversified offers.

Wellness & Relaxation

Tangier, with its combination of natural beauty and cultural depth, is ideal for people seeking wellness and leisure. Tangier has a number of choices to help you revitalize, whether you want to immerse yourself in the relaxing rituals of a traditional hammam, indulge in a lavish spa treatment, or simply relax on the beach. Here's a list of the top health and relaxation experiences in the city.

Traditional Hammams and Spa

Visiting a traditional Moroccan hammam is a must for anybody visiting Tangier. These public baths are an essential aspect of Moroccan culture, providing a distinct and intensely cleaning experience.

Hammam Al Hossoun: One of Tangier's most famous hammams, Hammam Al Hossoun provides a genuine experience. The treatment usually starts with a steam bath to open your pores, followed by a thorough exfoliation with black soap and a kessa glove. Finally, you will get a soothing rinse and massage. The hammam's calm environment and competent attendants provide a genuinely relaxing experience.

Hammam Al Hanafi: Located in the heart of Medina, Hammam Al Hanafi offers a traditional setting with stunning tile work and a peaceful atmosphere. Steam baths, exfoliating scrubs, and aromatherapy massages are among the services offered here. It is the best spot to relax and enjoy Moroccan hospitality.

Le Mirage Spa: The Le Mirage Spa, located in the luxury Le Mirage Hotel, offers a more opulent experience. The spa provides a variety of services, such as traditional hammam procedures, facials, body wraps, and massage. The exquisite atmosphere and competent service make it the ideal place for relaxation and pampering.

Yoga and Meditation Retreats

Tangier's tranquil scenery and quiet environs make an excellent setting for yoga and meditation. Whether you are an experienced practitioner or a beginner, you will find lots of ways to improve your well-being.

Yoga Tangier: This local studio provides a wide range of yoga sessions, including Vinyasa, Hatha, and Yin yoga. The expert teachers lead you through lessons that are appropriate for all skill levels, assisting you in achieving balance and inner serenity. The studio also offers classes and getaways, ensuring a complete wellness experience.

Villa Mandarine Yoga Retreat: This stunning villa, just a short drive from Tangier, provides intense yoga and meditation retreats. Daily yoga sessions, guided meditation, nutritious food, and trips to surrounding natural places are common features of these retreats. The quiet atmosphere and customized care make it an ideal choice for a relaxing vacation.

Moroccan Surf Adventures: Combines yoga with the pleasure of surfing. This one-of-a-kind weekend includes yoga classes to help you improve your flexibility and balance while surfing. The seaside environment and professional teachers make it an enjoyable and comprehensive approach to improve your physical and mental health.

Beachfront Relaxation Spots
Tangier's magnificent coastline is lined with lovely beaches that are ideal for relaxing and unwinding.

Plage Malabata: This quiet beach is famed for its golden beaches and crystal-clear seas. It is a great place to sunbathe, swim, or simply enjoy the sea wind. The beach is also surrounded with cafés and restaurants where you can have a meal or a cool drink while admiring the scenery.

Achakar Beach: Located near the Hercules Caves, Achakar Beach provides a more quiet and natural environment. The rough shoreline and breathtaking vistas make it an ideal location to unwind and reconnect with nature. Bring a book, go for a walk along the beach, or simply enjoy the tranquil atmosphere.

Cap Spartel: Although not a beach, Cap Spartel's beautiful cliffs and panoramic views of the Atlantic Ocean make it an ideal place to unwind. The region has various stunning overlooks and picnic areas where you may relax and enjoy Tangier's natural beauty.

Health and Fitness Centres

Tangier has various well-equipped health and fitness centers for individuals who want to keep up their exercise program while on vacation.

City Club Tangier: One of the city's major fitness centers, City Club Tangier has a variety of amenities, including a gym, swimming pool, and fitness classes. The club's sophisticated equipment and competent trainers ensure that you may maintain your training regimen while visiting Tangier.

Tangier Fit: A boutique fitness center that focuses on personal training and group fitness sessions. Tangier Fit offers a variety of exercise alternatives, including Pilates, yoga, high-intensity interval training (HIIT), and spinning. The friendly environment and attentive teachers make it an excellent location to keep active.

Le Mirage workout Center: Located in the Le Mirage Hotel, this workout center features cutting-edge equipment and a variety of wellness treatments. The facility features a gym, sauna, and indoor pool, giving you everything you need for a full exercise and relaxation experience.

Alternative Healing Practices

Tangier also provides a variety of alternative healing activities that can improve your general health and give a comprehensive approach to relaxing.

Reiki Tangier: Discover the advantages of Reiki, a Japanese practice for stress relief and relaxation. Reiki Tangier provides individual sessions in which a qualified practitioner employs gentle hand motions to channel energy and aid healing. It is a relaxing and restorative activity that may make you feel more balanced and at ease.

Aromatherapy & Essential Oils: Several local spas and wellness centers provide aromatherapy treatments that use essential oils. These therapies can help to reduce stress, boost mood, and increase general health. Aromatherapy, whether in the form of a massage or a bespoke oil combination, is a calming method to enhance your relaxation experience.

Acupuncture: For individuals interested in traditional Chinese treatment, there are various health clinics in Tangier that offer acupuncture. This technique entails placing small needles into precise spots on the body to promote healing and alleviate pain. Acupuncture treatments can assist with a variety of health concerns and improve your general sense of well-being.

In conclusion, Tangier's combination of natural beauty, cultural depth, and different health services makes it a great place to unwind and rejuvenate. Tangier offers endless possibilities to relax and rejuvenate your mind, body, and soul, whether you are bathing in a traditional hammam, doing yoga by the sea, or indulging in a lavish spa treatment. Accept the city's calm environment and allow it to take you to a state of complete relaxation.

Events & Festivals

Tangier is a city that comes alive with a variety of events and festivals every year. These festivals provide an opportunity to learn about the city's rich cultural legacy, creative expression, and civic spirit. Tangier has something for everyone, whether they enjoy traditional religious observances, exciting music and dance events, or cutting-edge art and film exhibitions. Here's an overview of Tangier's most prominent events and festivals.

Cultural Festivals

Tangier's cultural events give tourists an immersive experience by delving deeply into the city's history and artistic heritage.

Tangier International Book Fair: This yearly event brings together writers, publishers, and literary aficionados from around the world. The exhibition, held in the Tangier International Conference Center, will include book signings, readings, and conversations on a variety of themes. It is a must-see for anybody interested in literature or intellectual conversation.

Tanjazz Festival: The Festival, which celebrates the greatest of jazz music, is one of Tangier's most popular cultural events. Every September, the festival brings together worldwide and Moroccan jazz performers for a series of concerts at various locations across the city. The colorful atmosphere and high-quality performances make it a must-see on Tangier's cultural calendar.

National Festival of Popular Arts: This event celebrates traditional Moroccan arts and crafts, such as music, dancing, and storytelling. The festival, held in the ancient Kasbah and other notable locales, celebrates Moroccan history. Visitors may see performances by local artists, take part in workshops, and learn about traditional crafts and food.

Musical & Dance Festivals
Tangier's cultural identity is inextricably linked to music and dance, which are celebrated in a number of festivals.

Mediterranean Music Festival: The Festival honors the region's unique musical traditions. The event takes place in several locations throughout Tangier and involves performances by musicians from Spain, Italy, Greece, and Morocco. The broad blend of genres, together with the celebratory atmosphere, creates a one-of-a-kind cultural experience.

Tangier Electronic Music Festival: For electronic music aficionados, this event is a must-see. The event, which features performances by prominent DJs and electronic musicians from across the world, is held at some of Tangier's most iconic settings, such as beach clubs and historic sites. The high-energy music and breathtaking scenery make for an amazing experience.

Tangier Dance Festival: The Tangier Dance Festival is an annual event that brings together dancers from diverse disciplines, including modern, ballet, and traditional Moroccan dance. The festival features concerts, seminars, and contests, giving established and rising artists a chance to showcase themselves. It is an excellent opportunity to immerse yourself in Tangier's vibrant dance scene.

Arts and Film Festivals

Tangier has long been a destination for artists and filmmakers, and its festivals reflect this rich creative heritage.

Tangier International Film Festival: This famous festival celebrates the greatest of international cinema, with a special emphasis on films from the Arab world and Africa. Screenings take place in renowned locations including the Cinema Rif and the Tangier American Legation Museum. The festival also offers panel discussions, seminars, and networking opportunities for filmmakers and cinephiles.

Tangier Art Biennale: The Tangier Art Biennale, which takes place every two years, showcases contemporary art exhibitions, installations, and performances by international artists. The festival takes place in galleries and public areas around the city, converting it into a vivid canvas for artistic expression. It is a must-see event for art enthusiasts and anyone interested in current culture.

Tangier Photography Festival: This festival promotes the art of photography with exhibitions, seminars, and talks by well-known photographers. The event features a diverse spectrum of photographic techniques and themes, from documentaries to fine art. It is an excellent opportunity to learn about the visual narrative of Tangier and beyond.

Religious & Traditional Celebrations

Tangier's religious and traditional events provide insights into the city's spiritual and cultural life.

Eid al-Fitr, which marks the end of Ramadan, is a prominent event in Tangier. Families gather to pray, eat meals, and give presents. The city's streets and residences are decorated, and special activities and marketplaces are conducted to honor the occasion. It is a time of celebration and community solidarity.

Eid al-Adha, also known as the Festival of Sacrifice, is one of Islam's most significant feasts. The festival involves special prayers, feasts, and charitable gestures. Families customarily sacrifice a sheep or goat and share the flesh to family members, friends, and those in need. It is a highly important occasion that emphasizes the virtues of charity and compassion.

Moussem of Moulay Abdessalam: This yearly trip to the shrine of Moulay Abdessalam, a venerated Sufi saint, is a big deal for many Moroccans. The celebration features religious services, music, and social feasts. It provides a chance to immerse oneself in Moroccan spirituality and community.

Annual Events and Public Holidays.

Aside from the major festivals, Tangier organizes a number of yearly events and public holidays that add to the city's lively calendar.

King's Day: Celebrated on July 30th, to commemorate King Mohammed VI's entry to the throne. Parades, fireworks, and other public activities are held on this day. It is a patriotic holiday that emphasizes Moroccan pride and solidarity.

New Year's Eve: Tangier's New Year's Eve celebrations are vibrant and joyous. The city's pubs, restaurants, and clubs offer special events, while fireworks illuminate the night sky. It is an excellent opportunity to explore Tangier's nightlife and participate in the festivities.

Tangier Marathon: Held annually, the Tangier Marathon draws participants from all over the world. The race course brings runners through the city's picturesque streets, with breathtaking views of the Mediterranean and Tangier's ancient attractions. Whether you are a seasoned marathoner or a casual runner, this is a fun and exciting event.

In conclusion, Tangier's many events and festivals cater to a wide range of interests, from cultural enthusiasts and music fans to families and spiritual searchers. These events give not only entertainment and enjoyment, but also a better appreciation of the city's history and vibrant, cosmopolitan personality. When planning your trip to Tangier, be sure to include some of these dynamic events on your schedule to fully immerse yourself in the city's active and eclectic atmosphere.

Practical Information

Planning a vacation to Tangier entails more than simply knowing where to go and what to see. Understanding the practical aspects of travel, such as transportation, healthcare, local traditions, and handy terminology, may substantially improve your whole experience. This chapter contains all of the information you need to successfully traverse Tangier and enjoy a hassle-free holiday.

Transportation in Tangier

Tangier is very easy to navigate, due to a multitude of transit alternatives. Here's a guide that will help you travel the city efficiently:

Taxis: Taxis are a popular and easy method to get about Tangier. There are two sorts of taxis: Petit Taxis, which are small and often cover short distances inside the city, and Grand Taxis, which are larger and may transport you to locations outside of the city. Petit Taxis are metered, so ensure the driver activates the meter at the start of your journey. Grand Taxis operate on defined routes and charges, so you should agree on a fee before beginning your journey.

Buses: The Tangier public bus system is an inexpensive method to move about the city. The buses cover the majority of the key districts and tourist sites. While the service may not be as regular or punctual as in certain Western cities, it is an affordable choice for budget tourists.

Trains: Tangier is well connected to other major Moroccan cities via train. The Tangier Ville train station is modern and efficient, with daily services to Casablanca, Rabat, and Marrakech. The high-speed Al Boraq train is particularly remarkable, as it considerably reduces travel time between Tangier and Casablanca.

Car Rentals: If you prefer the freedom of driving, automobile rentals are available at both the airport and the city center. Renting a car is a fantastic alternative if you want to explore the surrounding areas, such as the Rif Mountains or adjacent seaside cities

Walking and Cycling: Tangier's tiny city center is suitable for strolling. Exploring on foot allows you to absorb up the ambiance and find hidden gems. Furthermore, some regions have bike rentals, which may be an enjoyable and environmentally beneficial way to explore the city.

Emergency Contacts & Healthcare

Being prepared for emergencies is essential when traveling. Here are some important contacts and healthcare suggestions.

Emergency Numbers:
- Police: 19.
- Ambulance: 15.
- Fire Department: 15

Hospitals And Clinics:
- **Tangier Regional Hospital** is Tangier's primary public hospital, providing a wide range of medical services.
- **Clinique de Tanger:** A private clinic noted for providing high-quality care and extensive medical services.
- **American Hospital of Tangier:** Another respected private hospital with top-notch facilities and English-speaking personnel.

Pharmacies are extensively available in Tangier, and many stay open late. Look for "Pharmacie de Garde" signage indicating after-hours service.

Travel Insurance: It is strongly advised to have travel insurance that covers medical emergencies, trip cancellations, and other unexpected situations.

Make sure your insurance coverage is valid in Morocco.

Local Customs & Etiquette

Respecting local traditions and etiquette is critical to ensuring a great experience and avoiding misunderstandings:

Greetings: Moroccans are famed for their hospitality. Greetings are a significant aspect of the culture. Handshakes are popular, and close friends or relatives may share cheek kisses. It is appropriate to use titles such as "Sidi" (Mr.) and "Lalla" (Mrs./Ms.) followed by the person's first name.

Dress Code: Although Tangier is rather liberal, it is customary to dress modestly, especially when visiting religious places or rural regions. For women, this includes covering their shoulders and knees. Men should not wear shorts in more conservative contexts.

Public Behavior: Public shows of affection are often discouraged. Holding hands is generally okay, but more personal gestures should be saved for private occasions.

Dining Etiquette: When dining with natives, it is traditional to wash your hands before eating. Food is generally shared from a communal dish, and eating with your right hand is considered courteous. Accepting food or drink, especially if it is a modest quantity, is considered gracious.

Bargaining: Haggling is common in marketplaces and souks. Begin with a low offer and progress to a mutually acceptable price. Maintain a positive and courteous tone throughout the encounter.

Useful Arabic & French Phrases

While many people in Tangier speak English, learning a few phrases in Arabic and French may enrich your experience and demonstrate respect for the local culture.

Arabic Phrases:
- Hello: Salam (سلام)
- Thank you: Shukran (شكراً)
- Please: Min fadlik (من فضلك)
- Yes: Naam (نعم)
- No: La (لا)

French Phrases:
- Hello: Bonjour
- Thank you: Merci

- Please: S'il vous plaît
- Yes: Oui
- No: Non

Getting Help:
- Do you speak English?: Parlez-vous anglais? (French), Hal tatakallam al-ingliziya? (Arabic) (هل تتكلم الإنجليزية؟)
- Where is...?: Où est...? (French), Ayna...? (Arabic) (أين...؟)
- How much is this?: Combien ça coûte? (French), Bikam hadha? (Arabic) (بكم هذا؟)

Final Travel Tips & Recommendations

Here are some extra ideas for a successful and pleasurable vacation to Tangier:

Travel Insurance: Make sure you have comprehensive travel insurance that covers health, accidents, and trip cancellation.

Local Currency: The Local currency is the Moroccan Dirham (MAD). It is important to carry some cash, particularly for little transactions and marketplaces. ATMs are widespread, and credit cards are accepted in the majority of hotels and restaurants.

Water Safety: It is advised to consume bottled water because tap water may not be safe for all travelers. Bottled water is widely accessible at stores and motels.

Electricity: Morocco utilizes the standard European 220V/50Hz electrical system. Make sure you have the correct adapters for your devices.

Time Zone: Tangier follows Greenwich Mean Time (GMT) during regular time and GMT+1 during daylight saving time. Plan your time appropriately.

Tipping: Tipping is traditional in Morocco. In restaurants, a 10-15% tip is appreciated. A few dirhams will be enough for modest services like porters and taxi drivers.

In conclusion, with these practical suggestions and crucial information, you will be well-prepared to appreciate everything Tangier has to offer. This book covers everything from efficient transit alternatives and emergency contacts to learning local customs and key terminology, so you may traverse Tangier with confidence and make the most of your vacation. For an unforgettable experience, embrace the city's rich culture, bustling events, and friendly welcome.

Sample Itineraries

Crafting the ideal itinerary can make all the difference between a good vacation and a great one. Whether you're in Tangier for a weekend, a full week, or a family vacation, this guide provides carefully curated itineraries to help you make the most of your time in this vibrant city. Let's dive into some sample itineraries tailored to different types of trips.

Weekend Getaway Itinerary
Day 1: Arrival and City Introduction
- Morning: Arrive in Tangier and check into your accommodation. Once settled, start your adventure with a visit to the Medina of Tangier. Wander through its narrow streets, soak in the vibrant atmosphere, and explore the bustling souks. Don't miss the chance to visit the Kasbah Museum, where you can learn about Tangier's rich history and enjoy panoramic views of the city and the Mediterranean Sea.

- Afternoon: Head to the Grand Socco, a lively square that serves as the gateway to Medina. Enjoy a leisurely lunch at a nearby café, sampling some traditional Moroccan dishes like tagine or couscous. After lunch, take a short walk to the American Legation Museum, an intriguing museum housed in the first American public property outside the United States.

- Evening: End your day with a stroll along the Corniche, the scenic coastal promenade. Find a cozy restaurant with a view of the sea and enjoy a delicious dinner while watching the sunset.

Day 2: Cultural and Natural Wonders
- Morning: Start your day with a traditional Moroccan breakfast, featuring fresh bread, honey, and mint tea. Then, make your way to the Caves of Hercules, located just outside the city. These fascinating caves are steeped in legend and offer a unique photo opportunity with their stunning rock formations.

- Afternoon: Head to Cape Spartel, where the Mediterranean Sea meets the Atlantic Ocean. Enjoy the breathtaking views and visit the historic lighthouse. Afterwards, return to the city and visit Perdicaris Park, a peaceful green space perfect for a relaxing walk or picnic.

- Evening: For your last evening in Tangier, immerse yourself in the local culture with a visit to a traditional hammam (bathhouse). After a rejuvenating spa experience, treat yourself to a dinner of fresh seafood at one of the city's renowned seafood restaurants.

One-Week Adventure Itinerary
Day 1: Arrival and Exploration
- Settle into your accommodation and spend your first day exploring the Medina and its key attractions, including the Kasbah Museum and the American Legation Museum. Enjoy a traditional Moroccan dinner to kick off your week-long adventure.

Day 2: Tangier's Highlights
- Spend the day visiting some of Tangier's must-see attractions, such as the Grand Socco, the Petit Socco, and the bustling souks. Enjoy a leisurely lunch at a local café, then head to the Tangier American Legation Museum. In the evening, take a sunset stroll along the Corniche.

Day 3: Day Trip to Asilah
- Take a day trip to the charming coastal town of Asilah, known for its beautiful murals and relaxed vibe. Explore the medina, visit the seaside ramparts, and enjoy fresh seafood by the sea. Return to Tangier in the evening and dine at a local restaurant.

Day 4: Nature and Adventure
- Start your day with a visit to the Caves of Hercules and Cape Spartel. In the afternoon, explore Perdicaris Park and enjoy a nature walk. For the adventurous, consider a camel ride along the beach. In the evening, relax with a traditional Moroccan meal.

Day 5: Cultural Immersion
- Immerse yourself in Tangier's cultural scene with a visit to St. Andrew's Church and the Tangier Cemetery. In the afternoon, participate in a Moroccan cooking class or a henna art workshop. Spend the evening enjoying live music at a local venue.

Day 6: Day Trip to Chefchaouen
- Embark on a day trip to the enchanting blue city of Chefchaouen. Wander through its picturesque streets, visit the kasbah, and

enjoy the stunning mountain views. Return to Tangier in the evening and savor a delightful dinner.

Day 7: Relaxation and Farewell
- Spend your final day relaxing at one of Tangier's beaches or enjoying a traditional hammam experience. Do some last-minute shopping for souvenirs at the souks. In the evening, have a memorable farewell dinner at a fine dining restaurant.

Family Vacation Itinerary
Day 1: Arrival and Relaxation
- Check into your family-friendly accommodation and spend the day exploring the Medina. Introduce the kids to the vibrant souks and enjoy a family meal at a local restaurant.

Day 2: Kid-Friendly Attractions
- Visit the Tangier Kasbah and the Kasbah Museum to give the children a taste of Tangier's history. In the afternoon, head to the Grand Socco and enjoy some ice cream from a local vendor. Spend the evening at Perdicaris Park, where the kids can run around and enjoy the playgrounds.

Day 3: Beach Day
- Take a day trip to one of Tangier's family-friendly beaches, such as Plage Achakar. Let the kids play in the sand and splash in the shallow waters. Pack a picnic or enjoy a beachside lunch at a nearby café. In the evening, return to the city and dine at a family-friendly restaurant.

Day 4: Educational Fun
- Visit the American Legation Museum and participate in a family-friendly tour. In the afternoon, explore St. Andrew's Church and the Tangier Cemetery, teaching the kids about different cultures and histories. For dinner, find a restaurant that offers Moroccan cuisine with kid-friendly options.

Day 5: Interactive Experiences
- Spend the day at one of Tangier's interactive exhibits or entertainment centers, such as a science museum or an aquarium. In the afternoon, take a family-friendly cooking class where everyone can learn to make traditional Moroccan dishes. Enjoy the fruits of your labor for dinner.

Day 6: Outdoor Adventures
- Head to the Caves of Hercules and let the kids explore the fascinating rock formations. Afterwards, visit Cape Spartel and enjoy the views from the lighthouse. In the afternoon, consider a camel or horseback riding experience, which the whole family will enjoy. End the day with a casual dinner at a beachside café.

Day 7: Farewell Tangier
- Spend your final day doing some last-minute shopping for souvenirs at the souks. Let the kids pick out their favorite mementos. Relax at a nearby park or playground before heading to the airport. For your last meal, choose a restaurant with a view of the sea to enjoy a family-friendly dinner.

In conclusion, these sample itineraries are designed to help you make the most of your time in Tangier, whether you're there for a short weekend, a full week, or a family vacation. With a mix of cultural experiences, natural beauty, and family-friendly activities, Tangier offers something for everyone. Use these itineraries as a guide, but feel free to tailor them to your interests and pace. Enjoy your journey in this vibrant and captivating city!

Conclusion

Tangier, with its intriguing mix of cultures, history, and natural beauty, serves as an enticing entryway to Morocco. This book has shown you the many sides of this dynamic city, from its bustling medinas and ancient sites to its peaceful beaches and picturesque scenery. As you prepare to wrap up your tour or plan your next excursion, consider the essential features and spirit of what makes Tangier a remarkable location.

Tangier's unusual location at the crossroads of Europe and Africa lends it a distinct character that is both cosmopolitan and truly Moroccan. The architecture, museums, and stories shared by inhabitants all reflect the city's rich past. Whether you were meandering around the Kasbah, visiting the American Legation Museum, or admiring the views from Cape Spartel, Tangier's historical significance is sure to leave an effect.

Tangier's cultural activities provide an intensive trip into both Moroccan traditions and modern manifestations. These activities, which range from a traditional Moroccan tea ceremony to a culinary lesson, allow a more in-depth connection to the local way of life. The city's strong cultural culture, which includes galleries and performances, exemplifies the creative spirit that flourishes here.

Nature enthusiasts have surely enjoyed Tangier's outdoor amenities. The city's coastline beauty, as demonstrated by the Caves of Hercules and the peaceful beaches, provide an ideal setting for leisure and adventure. The adjacent Rif Mountains and the lovely town of Chefchaouen provide further chances for travel and discovery.

Tangier provides a warm environment for families, with activities suitable for all ages. The parks, kid-friendly museums, and interactive displays keep younger visitors interested and amused.

Practical parts of your vacation, such as understanding local traditions, managing transit, and learning key words, will make your trip more pleasurable. Tangier's hospitality, as seen by warm greetings and polite exchanges, contributes to a positive overall vacation experience.

As you reflect on your journey to Tangier, keep in mind not just the sights you saw, but also the sounds, flavors, and moments of connection that made it memorable. Whether you're leaving the city or planning your next visit, Tangier's attraction and charm will stay with you. Safe travels, and may your journey be full of discovery and delight.

Printed in Great Britain
by Amazon